ENJOY TODAY:

A Daily Inspirational Book

AYOOLA KAFFO

DEDICATION

To Almighty God, my maker and creator. Thank You
God for the gift of Life.

CONTENTS

Foreword

Phenomenal facts of life flowing from the inspired mind of an enlightened soul

All potential readers of this book, 'Enjoy Today' will become, not only better informed, but move a notch higher than they were prior to reading this piece of amazing work.

I commend the author.

Dr Dele Owolawi, author of Dialogue with the Self.

Well Done.

Thanks for being a vessel of purposeful living.

Bisi Dada, Pastor RCCG Alpha Courts

Introduction

This book 'Enjoy Today' is a daily journal. It includes daily motivational quotes, inspiring words, affirmations and scriptural passages and phrases to help you kick start each day onto the right path.

In one of Lisa Nicholls's motivational videos, she mentions that "A great Life is made of Amazing Moments"! I believe that totally; and agree that a great life is made of amazing days and amazing moments, and that each day and every moment should be enjoyed to the fullest.

The journal is a compilation of quotes, words, principles, affirmations including reviews of books that I have read over the years which have served me well on my journey in life. Some aspects of this book/journal reflect my personal experiences, while some aspects include my thoughts for specific days; and lessons learnt from occurrences and events.

The story behind the book

The inspiration for 'Enjoy Today' is traced back to 2015, although my passion for reading and writing had developed many years before this. I was a speaker in 2015 during the 2-day national training event that my organisation holds every year. I spoke for about 12 minutes to an audience of 500 to 600 about a topic 'My Journey so Far – A Resilient Practitioner.' I was the last speaker for the 1st day and the feedback received was phenomenal. The audience received it well and many people came up to me afterwards to tell me they found the talk encouraging and inspiring.

The following day, the convener unexpectedly asked me to open the meeting for the day with some encouraging words. Being that it was also the first day of the month of July, I said something along the lines of – Its a new day, a new dawn, a new month, a new season, etc. It was equally very well received. My colleagues were impressed but surprised as to where that gift came from. On return to my workplace, I was again approached to write some words of advice to encourage and uplift the employees for the week, which was published in the weekly Bulletin.

After these events, I carried on as normal. A few months later, an opportunity to take up employment in the Middle East opened up. I accepted it willingly and cheerfully; painfully leaving a job I loved and my loving family in UK. I decided the best way to keep in regular touch with my 2 children will be to send them text/whatsapp messages every morning after my morning prayer. The message was to say good morning, a quote and word of prayer or encouragement. I always ended each message with 'Enjoy Today.' I sent the messages unfailingly every day since 20 April 2016.

My 18 year old daughter told an adult family friend about the messages I send her every morning, as one of the quotes I had sent related to what was being discussed at the time. The family friend then requested that I send the messages to her 2 children also, which I did from August 2016. In September 2016, I included my nephew, and another young adult family of my husband. I also included a friend, an Associate Professor for comments and feedback about the messages; increasing the number of people I send messages to daily up to 7.

So my duty every morning as part of my morning routine was to send motivational word/thought of the day to 7 people. The WhatsApp messages always ended with Enjoy Today, a smiley face, prayer sign and a thumb up sign. I did this faithfully everyday by God's grace and at the end of each month, I compiled the messages and saved them.

During a holiday trip in March 2017, I bought 3 books from a bookstore. One of the books – *You can Heal your Life* by Louise Hay, I had already read but gave the book away and wanted to replace and re-read it. The 2nd book was by Robin Sharma, *Be Extraordinary*. I had read a book by Robin recently – *The Monk who Sold His Ferrari*; and felt buying another of his book will be money well spent and reading another of his book will definitely be worthwhile. The 3rd book I picked and bought was by Jack Canfield and Ram Ganglani called *The Magical Book of Affirmations*. The book was on the shelf tightly wrapped up so I was unable to read inside the book whilst at the store. I opened it up the following morning and after reading the dedication page, it struck something so strong inside of me; an idea that had crossed my mind several times. I decided there and then that I will write not only one but three books. I wrote down the names of all the three books. The first one being 'Enjoy Today'!

I did not have my laptop with me at the time, but on paper right there, I was inspired to write the introduction of 'Enjoy Today', the story behind the book and the dedication. I already had been compiling and saving on a monthly basis the messages I send daily, not knowing at the time that I was saving it for the creation of a book that will be called 'Enjoy Today.'

That day 06 March 2017, I made an extraordinary decision and I took action. If you fast forward this journal to 06 March, you will notice the encouragement or word for that day. This was written about 40 minutes before I made the decision, which makes it truly Divine and Extraordinary.

With all gratitude to God, I thankfully present my impressions, inspirations and knowledge gathered over the year to you; and pray that it would be a pleasant and rewarding journey for all.

Enjoy 'Enjoy Today'

Ayoola Kaffo.

1
JANUARY – BE INSPIRED

01 January

Good Morning!

Glory to God, It's:

A New Day!
A New Dawn!
A New Week!

A New Month!
A New Year!
A New Beginning!

A New Season!

"Behold, I will do a new thing, now it shall spring forth; shall you not know it? I will even make a road in the wilderness and rivers in the desert" - Isa 43:19.

Thanking God for renewed hope and strength! Expect something new!

Enjoy Today

02 January

Good Morning!

Life is like a Book!
Every Day is a new Page
Every Month is a new Chapter
Every Year is a new Series.

What will be written in your page this new day?

What will be written in your chapter this new month?

What will be written in your series this New Year?

Make it Inspiring, Impactful and Interesting!

Enjoy Today

03 January

Good Morning!

People who tend to follow the Crowd, always get lost!

Let God's Word be the ultimate authority for your life!

Enjoy Today

28 January

Good Morning!

I came across a quote once that says, "The secret of Success is found in your daily routine" –unknown author. This is so true

What you do on a consistent basis can make or break you. Consistent actions have long term maximum effects!
Success and failure does not suddenly show up, it creeps in slowly by what you do or don't do!

Make sure your daily routine is one that serves you well.

Enjoy Today

29 January

Good morning!

You are designed to rule, reign and radiate in your area of gifting!

You are Valuable!

You are Worthy!
You are Significant!
You are Relevant!

As you step out today, be all that God has created you to be!

Enjoy Today

30 January

Good Morning!

Our Belief system is key to our achievements and greatness!

Your belief system comes from your ideas. You express outwardly the ideas in your head!

So, what ideas and beliefs do you have?

Are they ones that serve you well?

Enjoy Today

16 February

Good Morning!

"When obstacles arise, you change your Direction to reach your Goal; you do not change your Decision to get there" - Zig Ziglar.

Enjoy Today

17 February

Good Morning!

"The Secret of Getting Ahead is Getting Started" - Mark Twain

When you stop 'whining', and take action, you start winning!

Enjoy Today

18 February

Good Morning!

You are Outstanding!
You Stand Out!
You are Unique!
You are Different!

People are often drawn to us because of our differences, not our similarity. So don't try to be or wish you were someone else!
God has created each of us with unique gifts, personality, skills, capabilities and abilities! We also all have different experiences!

Enjoy Today

19 February

Good Morning!

It's a privilege to be alive! Be Grateful
Honor the giver of life.

Enjoy Today

20 February

Good Morning!

Today is Here and Now! I'm so Excited!
Make Today amazing! Enjoy Today

21 February

Good Morning!

It's a Great Day to be Alive!
I am Grateful to God and Truly Blessed!

Enjoy Today

22 February

Good Morning!

"Do all the good you can,
By all the means you can,
In all the ways you can,
In all the places you can,
At all the times you can,
To all the people you can,
As long as ever you can" - By John Wesley

Today be all you can.

Enjoy Today

23 February

Good Morning!

DO NOT WORRY!

Worrying does not take away tomorrow's troubles, it takes away Today's Peace!

Enjoy Today

24 February

Good Morning!

Health is Wealth!

A Sound mind, a sound body and a nourished soul make a healthy life!

Enjoy Today

25 February

Good Morning!

What you Think you Become,
What you Feel you Attract

What you Imagine you create!

Enjoy Today

26 February

Good Morning!

There is a time and place for everything!
This is the time to Arise and Shine!

Enjoy Today

27 February

Good Morning!

"Though no one can go back and make a brand new
start, anyone can start from now and make a brand
new ending" - Carl Bard

This is so true; what's done is done. We can't go back
and undo choices we made. We can however, pause,
and make smarter decisions and choices to create
something better. Start Now. Enjoy Today

28 February

Good Morning!

Success is about becoming the best version of yourself!

Enjoy Today

29 February (For Leap Year Only)

Good Morning!

This day only comes around once every four years on a leap year.

Believe it or not, I was born on this very day!!

That makes me very unique and special! But we all are.

Enjoy Today

3
MARCH – DON'T QUIT

01 March

Good Morning!

It's a New Month!

Stay Empowered

Be Encouraged

I pray that God guide and direct your path this month and beyond. Amen

Enjoy Today

02 March

Good Morning!

No matter what knocks you down in life, get back up and keep going.

Just keep on keeping on!

Enjoy Today

03 March

Good Morning!

Every Day is a New Beginning!
Take a deep breath and be grateful for Today!
Step out boldly and make proper use of Today.

Be Phenomenal
Be Remarkable
Be Extraordinary

Enjoy Today

04 March

Good Morning!

The earth is governed by Principles.
You reap what you sow!

Enjoy Today

05 March

Good Morning!

On a recent flight from Dubai to Riyadh, I watched a movie called 'Me Before You'.
It's a story about Lou and Will and I cried watching the last scene.
If you look beyond the romance; there are a whole load of Life Lessons to be learnt from the movie.

I want to share what Will said to Lou at the end, as this is definitely recommended for all:

Live boldly
Push yourself
Don't settle
Live well
Just Live - LIVE.

Enjoy Today

06 March

Good Morning!

As you rise up this morning;
Raise above Average!
Raise above Mediocrity!

Be Extraordinary!
Be Outstanding!

There is more in you than you think or know.
There is more to life!

Enjoy Today

07 March

Good Morning!

Today is a Wonderful Day.
I choose to make it so.
All is well in my World!

Enjoy Today

08 March

Good Morning!

Take some time today to think about Freedom and what it means to you!

Remember it is important above all to be free from fear and the limitations we place on ourselves.

Set yourself free!

Enjoy Today

09 March

Good Morning!

Tough times don't last, tough people do!

"---Be Strong in the Lord and in the Power of His Might---" – (Eph 6:10a)

Enjoy Today

10 March

Good Morning!

Each Day we have the opportunity to make choices.
The way we choose shapes our destiny!
Choose wisely! Don't React, Respond!

Enjoy Today

11 March

Good Morning!

I am so Grateful for my Life!
I am so Grateful to be Alive!

It feels great to be Alive!

Despite my past, challenges and experiences, what matters most is I'm fully Alive and living.

Life is definitely worth living!

Enjoy Today

12 March

Good Morning!

Life is Wonderful. Be Excited!

Put a smile on your face!

Enjoy Today

13 March

Good Morning!

There is always light at the end of the tunnel!

With this in mind, just keep on moving!!

Enjoy Today

14 March

Good Morning!

Life is such an amazing gift!

Enjoy Today

15 March

Good Morning!

You don't have to be Great to Start; but you have to Start to be Great!

Take the necessary action
Just Do It!

Enjoy Today

16 March

Good Morning!

It does not matter how slowly you go, so long as you don't stop!

Keep Moving
Keep Going
Keep Growing

Enjoy Today

17 March

Good Morning!

Every action in the present prepares us for the Future!

Be Prepared!

Enjoy Today

18 March

Good morning!

The place of Positive Affirmations in our lives can't be quantified. Whatever we pronounce after the words 'I am' is what will be!

What we say to ourselves matter a great deal!

Enjoy Today

19 March

Good Morning!

Don't let fear, assumptions and negative beliefs stop you. Be the Best you can!

Enjoy Today

20 March

Good Morning!

"Life begins at the end of your 'Comfort Zone" – Neale Donald Walsch.

You don't change when comfortable.
You don't grow in comfort
You don't improve in comfort zone
You don't learn anything new in a comfort zone.

When you grow, improve, change/make a change, and learn; you are actually living!

So step out of your comfort zone, challenge yourself and truly live!

Enjoy Today.

21 March

Good Morning!

Whatever you focus on expands!
Energy flows where your attention goes!

Focus on the positive, not the negative.
Focus on your goals not your holes.
Focus on what you want, not want you don't want.

Enjoy Today.

22 March

Good Morning!

Thank you Lord!

"I will bless the Lord at all times; His praise shall
continually be in my mouth" - Psalm 34:1

Enjoy Today.

23 March

Good Morning!

Arise and Shine!
You are a Victor not a Victim!

Enjoy Today.

24 March

Good Morning!

I visited Dubai for the second time two weeks ago.
There were two places I was keen to re-visit; the
Dancing Fountain and the foyer of the hotel I stayed
the first time. Why you may ask?
I rushed through the experience the first time. I was
too busy taking pictures that I did not enjoy the best
part of being there.

It was different the second time around, I spent more
time by the fountain, to capture the half hourly music
that brings the atmosphere and surroundings alive. It
was breathtaking!
I listened; I danced slowly and enjoyed every moment
of the 6 minute music. I took one or two pictures, but
that was not my focus.

My focus was to be in the moment and totally enjoy
the experience.

I also re-visited Rove Hotel. The hotel's foyer has a very nice compelling aroma. It may be insignificant to many but for me, it was a brilliantly beautiful place to be. I went back to the hotel just for that aroma and I had a smile on my face walking into that hotel. I soaked in the environment and it was so amazing. I will not be forgetting that in a while.

I learnt a great lesson from both experiences. You see, in life we cannot go back to experience yesterday. My second time experience was not the same as the first. Those moments have gone forever!
We need to slow down, get rid of distractions and just enjoy each and every moment. It's possible to be in a place and not be there! Don't rush through Life, you will miss amazing moments.

Enjoy Today.

25 March

Good Morning!

"Life is not about the steps we have taken but about the Footprints we have left behind" –unknown author.

What footprints or impressions are you leaving behind?

Enjoy Today.

26 March

Good Morning!

You cannot discover new oceans unless you have courage to lose sight of the shore!

Sometimes having a plan B does not help.

Enjoy Today

27 March

Good Morning!

If you are not getting the right results, then it's time to change the way you do things. There is no better day to do that, than today!

Enjoy Today

28 March

Good Morning!

Don't get caught up in what others say about you!

What you think, say and believe about yourself is what matters most!

Enjoy Today

29 March

Good Morning!

You have so much to live for.

Hold on!

Enjoy Today

30 March

Good Morning!

Some people will speak for you.
Some people will speak about you.
Some people will speak against you.

The bottom line is people will always speak!
Regardless of what is said; don't allow it to determine the pace of your life!

Keep moving ahead!

Enjoy Today

31 March

Good Morning!

There is Power in Prayer.

Talk to God!

Enjoy Today

4
APRIL – IMPOSSIBLE IS NOTHING

01 April

Good Morning!

Glory to Almighty God!

It's a New Day, a New Dawn, a New Week, a new Month, a New Beginning and a New Season!

Do something New!

"I can do all things through Christ who strengthens me" - Phil 4:13

Be Empowered!

Enjoy Today

02 April

Good Morning!

It's a New Day.
Each day is an opportunity.
This day has never existed before!

Be Excited.
Step out and enjoy to the fullest!

Enjoy Today

03 April

Good Morning!

"God is my refuge and strength; a very present help in time of need" - Psalm 46:1.

God is with you. Step out with boldness!

Enjoy Today

04 April

Good Morning!

Everything happens for a reason; and good things come from challenging experiences!

Don't Quit!
Enjoy Today.

05 April

Good Morning!

Every setback is a setup for a comeback!

Be Encouraged!

Enjoy Today

06 April

Good Morning!

Actions open doors, consistency keep them open!
Do a little every day.
Do something every day.

Enjoy Today

07 April

Good Morning!

Every Day is a great day to be alive!

Be Excited!

Enjoy Today

08 April

Good Morning!

Yesterday I experienced one of my dreams/ goals

beginning to unfold right before my eyes. It was such an exhilarating feeling!

I sat for hours lost in time, doing what I enjoyed most with strength, happiness, empowerment, hope, joy and energy oozing out of me.

I remembered between August 2007 and Feb 2008, when I was at my lowest point, in pain and hurting so bad. The more I listened to Marvin Sapp's songs from a CD I purchased at the time, the more pain and helpless I felt.

9 years on, I'm sitting here with Yolanda Adams music playing in the background; and I'm so grateful to God. I know I am blessed & it's because of God that I even have Life.

The future is bright and colourful and I'm so excited!

Whatever it is you are going through; remember God is with you and working things out.

You are work in progress! Endure and hold on!

Enjoy Today

09 April

Good Morning!

Glory to God for a new Day!
Wake up and live!

Enjoy Today

10 April

Good Morning!

John 3:16

You are loved, you are saved and you are blessed.

Enjoy Today

11 April

Good Morning!

Glory to God!
I am Alive!
I am Well!
I am Standing!
I am Grateful for my Life
I am Grateful to be Alive!

Gratitude is the Best Attitude!

Enjoy Today.

12 April

Good Morning!

This was forwarded to me yesterday by a friend.

A lovely little girl was holding two apples with both hands.

Her mum came in and softly asked her little daughter with a smile; my sweetie, could you give your mum one of your two apples?

The girl looked up at her mum for some seconds, then she suddenly took a quick bite on one apple, and then quickly on the other.

The mum felt the smile on her face freeze. She tried hard not to reveal her disappointment.

Then the little girl handed one of her bitten apples to her mum, and said: mummy, here you are. This is the sweeter one. Wow!

No matter who you are, how experienced you are, and how knowledgeable you think you are, always delay judgement.

Give others the privilege to explain themselves.

What you see may not be the reality. Never conclude for others.

Which is why we should never only focus on the surface and judge others without understanding them first. Enjoy Today

13 April

Good Morning!

"Our eyes are placed in front because it more important to look ahead than to look back" - Warren

Buffett.

The past is in the past. Enjoy Today

14 April

Good Morning!

Be open to what God is doing and about to do in your life!

Enjoy Today.

15 April

Good Morning!

Glory to God for a new Day!
Thanking God for today, yesterday and all days.

Enjoy Today

16 April

Good Morning!

Be Grateful for your Life!

I have just finished reading a book titled 'A Thousand Splendid Suns' by Khaled Hosseini.
I came across it 3 days ago from a friend and

colleague who received it from a taxi driver, whose first language is not English. The book written in English was of no benefit to the driver so he gave it to my colleague.

I took the book just to glance through it, but I got hooked from the 1st page.
I will spare you the full details of the story, which is based on true events; centred around the lives of 2 girls and their journey in life.

All I can say to sum up this deeply moving book is: if you think your life is hard, think again! Someone out there prays for just a tiny fraction of what you have!

Be grateful!
You are blessed!

Enjoy every moment of your experiences!

Enjoy Today

17 April

Good morning!

A little progress each day adds up to big results!

Enjoy Today

18 April

Good Morning!

I am a child of God
I belong to the family of God
I am a shining star!

It is a new day and Jesus is Lord!
Happy Easter!

Enjoy Today

19 April

Good Morning!

Everything comes down to the choices we have and
the decisions we make!

Choose Wisely.

Enjoy Today

20 April

Good Morning!

Today is a Special Day!

You have the power to make it as awesome as you
want.

Create something special today.

Make an impact, make a difference; leave a good impression with everyone you come across.
Most importantly, just enjoy the day!

Enjoy Today

21 April

Good Morning!

Today is the right day to
Love
Learn
Laugh
Live

Enjoy Today

22 April

Good Morning!

It's a new Day!

Be wise to be Grateful!

Be courageous to be Happy!

Enjoy Today.

23 April

Good Morning!

Sometimes you Win!
Sometimes you Learn!

Enjoy Today.

24 April

Good Morning!

Just think about all the things you have that money
can't buy!
Count them and then make a conclusion about your
status!

I counted mine and I'm still counting; my outcome is
this:
I am Rich
I am Blessed
I am Grateful

Enjoy Today.

25 April

Good Morning!

It's so easy to take for granted things we have; and the people around us!

Pay more attention, give attention to what you have, what's around you and the people God has blessed you with!

So the things we are granted are not taken!

Enjoy Today

26 April

Good Morning!

It's a New Day!
Be Open to see Opportunities!
Be Sure to Enjoy every moment!

Enjoy Today.

27 April

Good Morning!

Glory to God, the giver of life!
The future is bright!
So is Today

Enjoy Today.

28 April

Good Morning!

Be Determined
Be Focused
Be Motivated
Be Inspired
Be Encouraged
Be Disciplined.

You are Equipped for Success.
Be all that God has created you to be!

Enjoy Today.

29 April

Good Morning!

Thank you Lord!
...."but by the Grace of God I am what I am....."

I am divinely Guided!
I am divinely Protected!

Thank God for His Grace and Mercy.

Enjoy Today

30 April

Good Morning!

Life is like photography, we develop from the negatives!

You are work in progress!

Enjoy Today

5
MAY – IMPOSSIBLE IS JUST A BIG WORD

01 May

Good Morning!

The decisions and choices we make are so crucial!

Yesterday I was reminiscing about the last 12 months. It was such a great feeling to remember and think back to all the happy memories and moments in the past year of my journey in life. It's a wonderful experience!

Now this is what made me pause; I could have missed it, if I did not make a move.

What if I didn't take that bold step on 07 April 2016

What if I let fear get the best of me?
What if I chose to stay in my familiar environment?
What if I chose 'the known' over the 'unknown'?
What if I listened to all the negative reports from people?
What if I did not take the risk?

What IF?

It's better to look back and say, 'I can't believe I did that' than to look back and say 'I wish I did that'.

It's a brand new month, the 5th month of the year. Just do it!

Enjoy Today

02 May

Good Morning!

It's a new day.
Embrace it with Gratitude!

Enjoy Today

03 May

Good Morning!

No person is rich enough to buy back the past.
Enjoy each moment before it is beyond your reach!

There is joy in each moment.

Enjoy Today

04 May

Good Morning!

No Pain, No Gain!
It may not be easy.
It will not be easy, but it will definitely be worth it!

Enjoy Today

05 May

Good Morning!
If you are always racing to the next moment, the next day, the next phase; what happens to the one you're in?

Enjoy Today.

06 May

Good Morning!

At every point of your life's journey, think about your

decisions, your actions, your behaviours and the choices you make!

What are you doing right now?
Is it Building you or Breaking you?
Is it Making you or Marking you?
You need Courage to Choose Wisely!

Be Encouraged! Enjoy Today

07 May

Good Morning!

Yesterday whilst I was dressing up for work, an old song dropped in my mind.
After work, I went on YouTube to search for it - Title: 'There's no stopping us - no one does it better' by Ollie and Jerry.
When I listened to it, it brought back so many memories. It put a big smile on my face. It was out in 1984 and I was 16 years at the time, but it was in vogue most of the 80s.

It transported me back to those times. I could feel the feelings I felt back then about life, the uplifting, the excitement as a young girl and all my big dreams.

My only regret is I wish I enjoyed those times and moments more.

The majority of us spend a big chunk of time worrying about things out of our control.

Sitting down here now and listening to that piece of music over again reminds me that despite all, those were brilliant and wonderful times that cannot be brought back.

Why am I telling you this? I am sharing this because I want you to enjoy Today, enjoy the Present, capture the moments, experience Now. Today Matters! Be happy on each step of your journey in life regardless. Tomorrow is unknown, yesterday is gone. Today is a gift!

Enjoy Today.

08 May

Good Morning!

The best place to be right now is in the Present.
You are here, alive and present!
Arise!
Be excited!
Enjoy each moment!
Life is beautiful. Smile.

Enjoy Today

09 May

Good Morning!

Today has something great in store for you!

Don't get caught up by what happened yesterday; but be captivated by the wonders of Today!

Enjoy Today.

10 May

Good Morning!

I read this brilliant article yesterday, which was forwarded by a friend.

The author is unknown, but I just had to share

I concluded after reading it that: What you do is not really important; it's how you do it!!

I was waiting in line for a ride at the airport in Dubai. When a cab pulled up, the first thing I noticed was that the taxi was polished to a bright shine. Smartly dressed in a white shirt, black tie, and freshly pressed black slacks, the cab driver jumped out and rounded the car to open the back passenger door for me.

He handed me a laminated card and said: 'I'm Abdul,

your driver. While I'm loading your bags in the trunk I'd like you to read my mission statement.'

Taken aback, I read the card. It said: Abdul's Mission Statement:
To get my customers to their destination in the quickest, safest and cheapest way possible in a friendly environment.

This blew me away. Especially when I noticed that the inside of the cab matched the outside. Spotlessly clean!

As he slid behind the wheel, Abdul said, 'Would you like a cup of coffee? I have a thermos of regular and one of decaf.'

I said jokingly, 'No, I'd prefer a soft drink.'

Abdul smiled and said, 'No problem. I have a cooler up front with regular and Diet Coke, Lassi (savoury drink), water and orange juice.'

Almost stuttering, I said, 'I'll take a Lassi.'

Handing me my drink, Abdul said, 'If you'd like something to read, I have The Star and Sun Times today.'

As we were pulling away, Abdul handed me another laminated card, 'These are the stations I get and the music they play, if you'd like to listen to the radio.'

And as if that weren't enough, Abdul told me that he had the air conditioning on and asked if the temperature was comfortable for me.

Then he advised me of the best route to my destination for that time of day. He also let me know that he'd be happy to chat and tell me about some of the sights or, if I preferred, to leave me with my own thoughts.

'Tell me, Abdul ,' I was amazed and asked him, 'have you always served customers like this?'

Abdul smiled into the rear view mirror. "No, not always. In fact, it's only been in the last two years. My first five years driving, I spent most of my time complaining like all the rest of the cabbies do. Then I heard about POWER OF CHOICE one day."

The Power of choice is that you can be a duck or an eagle.

'If you get up in the morning expecting to have a bad day, you'll rarely disappoint yourself. Stop complaining!'

'Don't be a duck. Be an eagle. Ducks quack and complain. Eagles soar above the crowd.'

'That hit me. really hard' said Abdul.

'It is about me. I was always quacking and complaining, so I decided to change my attitude and become an eagle.

I looked around at the other cabs and their drivers. The cabs were dirty, the drivers were unfriendly, and the customers were unhappy.

So I decided to make some changes, slowly ... a few at a time. When my customers responded well, I did more.'

'I take it that it has paid off for you,' I said.

'It sure has,' Abdul replied. 'My first year as an eagle, I doubled my income from the previous year. This year I'll probably quadruple it. My customers call me for appointments
on my cell phone or leave a message on it.'

Abdul made a different choice. He decided to stop quacking like a duck and start soaring like an eagle.

Start becoming an eagle today ... one small step every week..next week... And next...And....

Thought for today......

"You don't die if you fall in water, you die only if you

don't swim. That's the Real Meaning of Life.

Improve yourself and your skills in a different way.

Be an EAGLE.

Enjoy Today

11 May

Good Morning!

Mistakes are proof that you are trying!

Don't let it make you bitter

Let it make you better!

Try again.

Enjoy Today

12 May

Good Morning!

A little girl was once asked what she wants to be when she grows up. She replied 'To be Happy'. That about sums up Life - Be Happy! Enjoy Today.

13 May

Good Morning!

I love this quote by Abraham Lincoln. "The Best thing about the Future is that it comes One Day at a Time".

It's worth always remembering that the future does not come rushing at us. It comes in 'Daily Doses'; so we need to deal with life one day at a time. One of those days is Today, Here and Now!

Get fully engaged in the day at hand
Enjoy all the day has to offer
Cherish every moment
Make the most of Today
Start the day with gratitude, continue in gratitude and end the day with gratitude.

The future and our life truly comes one day at a time. Don't miss it!

Enjoy Today

14 May

Good Morning!

It's a new day for a fresh beginning!

Be better today than you were yesterday!

So as you awake this morning;
Be grateful that you are alive
Rise up
Step Out and Step Up!

Enjoy Today

15 May

Good Morning!

Glory to God for Life.

You are worthy of the very best in life!

Go ahead and enjoy life to the fullest.

Enjoy Today

16 May

Good Morning!

I am Bright

I am Beautiful
I am Colourful
I am Radiant
I am Outstanding
I am Illumination!

I Arise, I shine; for my light has come and the glory of the Lord has risen upon me. (Isaiah 60:1)

Enjoy Today

17 May

Good Morning!

I like to share my wonderful experience with you.
Yesterday I stumbled across a very powerful South African worship song, by Neyi Zimu titled Jeso Rato La Hao.
I did not understand the language of course, but I was so touched by it.
I found the translation later and it made it so meaningful!
God is worthy of worship!

I listened to it several times!
It is an Absolutely Amazing Holy Spirit Inspiring Uplifting South African Worship! A beautiful song indeed!

They showed great passion for worshiping God. Everyone was oozing with dancing and Joy. From the backup singers to the drummer, other worshippers on the stage to the audience. I certainly joined in! It must have been electrifying to be in that atmosphere!!

As you embark on your daily activities today, just remember all what God has done and is still doing for you; And worship Him anyway you know how!

Enjoy Today

18 May

Good Morning!

The Lord will perfect that which concerns you....
(Psalm 138: 8a). Enjoy Today

19 May

Good Morning!

Everything is working out for your Highest Good!

Be Calm
Be Cool
Be Confident!

Enjoy Today

20 May

Good Morning!

Sometimes some things won't make sense. Just remember God is Sovereign!

Hold on to your Faith!
Don't ever lose Hope!
Do look on the bright side of life!

Enjoy Today

21 May

Good Morning!

Keep Going, keep moving, and keep progressing.

But be mindful of the Now.

Enjoy Today

22 May

Good Morning!

Your life is your message to the world!

Make sure it's inspiring.

Enjoy Today

23 May

Good Morning!

It's a New Day!

Don't look back
Look Ahead!
Most importantly, look Around!

Enjoy Today

24 May

Good Morning!

'If you cannot do great things, do small things in a

great way' - Napoleon Hill.

Enjoy Today

25 May

Good Morning!

Whenever I see another breaking of the Day; I say Thank You Lord!

Enjoy Today.

26 May

Good Morning!

Waking up is a Blessing!
Life is a Blessing!
I am a Blessing!
I am Blessed and so are you!

Enjoy Today

27 May

Good Morning!

I may not be where I want to be, but I am not where I used to be!!
How Marvellous!

Look at how far you have come, rather than how far you have to go. You are doing great. Be thankful!

Enjoy Today

28 May

Good Morning!

You are created in the image of God; equipped for success
You are Empowered
You are the blessed and highly favored child of the Most High God

You are an Overcomer
You are a Winner
You are a Champion

You are Victorious
You are a Conqueror
You are Illumination
You are Radiant

You are Colourful

You are all that and a whole lot more!

Enjoy Today

29 May

Good Morning!

Take time to appreciate and enjoy the simple things in Life!

Enjoy Today

30 May

Good Morning!

It's a new day

Focus on your goal!

Don't be disturbed, distracted or discouraged

Enjoy Today

31 May

Good Morning!

There are some things we don't like to do, but should be done to bring about improvement or changes in our lives.

Now is the time to make the necessary changes you need to make to get your life in line. Just Do it!

Enjoy Today

6
JUNE – DREAM BIG

01 June

Good Morning!

It's a New Month!

Today is God's Day.
It is a good day!
I declare Today and all its activities good in the mighty name of Jesus.

Enjoy Today

02 June

Good Morning!

The earth is my dominion!
I rule by the Power of God
Therefore the earth shall continually yield the best for me in Jesus' name.

Enjoy Today

03 June

Good Morning!

"Cause me to hear your loving kindness in the morning, For in You do I trust; Cause me to know the way in which I should walk, For I lift up my soul to You". Psalm 143:8

Enjoy Today

04 June

Good Morning!

There is greatness in you!
You are unlimited.
Don't limit yourself.
Don't limit God!
All things are possible to whom who believes.

Enjoy Today

05 June

Good Morning!

Confess Daily!
I am God's Masterpiece
I am God's Most Priced Possession
I am Special
I am Significant
I am Relevant
I am all that God has created me to be.
I am fulfilling God's plan and purposes for my life.
I am making a positive impact in my generation and in my world!
In Life and Destiny I will make it!

Enjoy Today

06 June

Good Morning!

Lord I thank You for my Life!
I am grateful for what I have, grateful for what I had, grateful for what I have now and grateful for what I will have!

Let's Thank God:
I am Alive
I am Grateful to God for Life!

I am Safe
I am Grateful to God for Security!
I am Well
I am Grateful to God for Divine Health!
I am Strong, Able and Calm
I am Grateful to God for Power and Peace of Mind!
I am Healthy, Dynamic and Fully Alive
I am grateful to God for His Grace----But by the Grace of God, I am what I am (1 Cor 15: 10a)

Enjoy Today.

07 June

Good Morning!

But by the Grace of God; I am what I am... (1 Cor 15:10a)

I'm excited, today is my NEBOSH IGC exam day.

Ten years ago, I could not afford the course and exam! I also wasn't managing my time properly; and thought I could not fit it into my busy schedule!!

Things are different now. Glory to God!

From September 2016 till now, I have truly and thoroughly enjoyed the course and preparation towards this important exam. I intend to carry on in the same attitude today as I sit and write the exam.

All I can say is that, I pray you have such an exciting and enjoying day today too in whatever you do!

Enjoy Today

08 June

Good Morning!

Happiness is a Journey, not a Destination!
It's a Choice!
Enjoy the unnoticeable special moments that every day offers!
There is joy in the Process!

A very special birthday greeting to my Sister, Sade.

Enjoy Today

09 June

Good Morning!

Be inspired.
Be Passionate!
Passion is the fire that fuels your dreams.

Enjoy Today

10 June

Good Morning!

Be Bold!
Be Courageous!
Be Confident!
Be Fearless!
When you conquer your fears, you conquer your life!

For God has not given us a spirit of fear, but of love, of power and of a sound mind'(2 Tim 1:7).
You are blessed.

Enjoy Today

11 June

Good Morning!

Whatever the mind can believe and conceive, you can achieve!
You are equipped for Success!!

Enjoy Today

12 June

Good Morning!

You are Empowered!
Go ahead and fulfil your destiny
"I can do all things through Christ who strengthens
me"' (Phil 4:13).

Enjoy Today

13 June

Good Morning!

'I will praise You, for I am fearfully and wonderfully
made; marvellous are Your works, And that my soul
knows very well'. (Psalm 139:14).

Enjoy Today

14 June

Good Morning!

Our Identity determines in large measures Our
Destiny!

Your belief about 'who' and 'what' you think you are,
will affect the choices and decisions you make; and this

will affect your path in life!
So know who you are.

Enjoy Today

15 June

Good Morning!

Daily Positive Affirmations:

I am a blessed and Highly Favoured Child of the Most
High God!
I am God's most priced possession
I am God's Masterpiece
I am Special
I am Whole, Perfect, Complete, and Vibrant.
I am a Radiant Being enjoying life to the fullest.
I move through life knowing that I am Safe, Divinely
Guided and Divinely Protected.
I am all that God has created me to be!

Enjoy Today.

16 June

Good Morning!

It is Great to be alive!
Embrace life

Embrace your life!
Success on the outside begins with success on the inside!
It is the 'World Within' that makes the 'World Without'!
Let your thoughts, feelings and imagery/ imagination be ones that serve you!

Enjoy Today.

17 June

Good Morning!

Never lose Hope!

We need HOPE to COPE!

Enjoy Today

18 June

Good Morning!

There are 2 days of the year that you can do nothing about: Yesterday and Tomorrow!

You can do so much with Today!

Make every moment count! Enjoy Today

19 June

Good Morning!

Readers are Leaders!

Who is a Leader?

- Someone who reads and puts into practice habits and principles learnt in order to improve themselves.

- Someone who is keen on personal development and development in all areas of Life.

- Someone whose lifestyle, actions and words influences others positively.

Invest in yourself! Read and Lead!

Enjoy Today

20 June

Good Morning!

Life is a Journey with experiences to Enjoy!

Enjoy Today

21 June

Good Morning!

There is potential in you waiting to be unleashed!

Life has a lot to offer!

So keep moving, do more! Start now. Enjoy Today

22 June

Good Morning!

Arise and Smile!

Only good lies before you!

Only great things lie ahead!

Be Expectant!

Enjoy Today

23 June

Good Morning!

Be Grateful.
You are unique and special!
Be yourself
Never live your life for anybody
Appreciate what God has given you.

Appreciate what you have and where you are, on the way to where you ought to be.
Enjoy the journey, celebrate along the way and continue to trust God as you work towards a better life!

Enjoy Today

24 June

Good Morning!

All will be well. Life is Good!

Enjoy Today

25 June

Good Morning!

East or West, Home is the Best!

There is no place like home!

Enjoy Today

26 June

Good Morning!

Arise and Shine

You are a Star

Be all that God has created you to be!

Enjoy Today

27 June

Good Morning!

The largest room in the world is the room for improvement.

Enjoy Today

28 June

Good Morning!

Yesterday I watched King Women - Episode 10, as recommended by my niece. It is a video clip featuring the interview of a successful American born Nigerian Stylist and Fashion icon.

She narrated her life story; and she spoke of the highs

and lows of her life.

It was a great insight into her life, one that you would not have expected.

She talked about her struggles and sufferings encountered especially as a child and young woman; and how it's made her into the person she is today. It was a sad but beautiful and inspiring story; that left me to conclude (although I already knew this) that Life and Success is a Process and a Journey.

Despite ALL she went through, she did not allow her situation to define her! It worked for her in a big way!

Life lessons to learn: Never let your situation define who you are!

We are all destined to succeed but our choices, decisions and actions is key to its fulfilment.

Enjoy Today

29 June

Good Morning!

Difficult roads often lead to beautiful destinations, only if you keep moving!

Enjoy Today

30 June

Good Morning!

If it doesn't challenge you, it won't change you.

Great change and transformation awaits you when you move out of your comfort zone

So feel the fear and do it anyway!

Enjoy Today

7
JULY – RISE ABOVE AVERAGE

01 July

It's a New Month and a New Season of Prosperity, Abundance, Health and Success!

Expect Big!
Believe Big!
Think Big!
Dream Big!
Our God is Bigger!

Enjoy Today

02 July

Good Morning!

"As a man thinks in his heart, so is he". (Proverbs 23:7a).

Your thinking fuels Your World!
Your words frame Your World!
Think Accurately
Think Creatively
Think Positively
It's a new day, develop a new mindset. Think anew
and see a new you evolve!

Enjoy Today

03 July

Good Morning!
God loves you!
In all things, put first things first!

Make God Priority.
Acknowledge, Appreciate and Adore God!

Enjoy Today

04 July

Good Morning!

It's a wonderful day!

Thank God for life!

Every event offers you lessons!

There is a purpose for everything that has ever happened and for everything that will happen!

Enjoy the Day

05 July

Good Morning!

Basically, we owe it all to God!
Gods Grace and Mercy is the reason we are alive!
God's Power upholds us
God's Spirit directs us!
Be Grateful to God!
Be Grateful for life!
Be Grateful for God's love!

Enjoy Today

06 July

Good Morning!

God is Good!
God loves you!

God is with you!
God knows what you are going through!
God cares for you!
God has a good plan for you!

Enjoy Today

07 July

Good Morning!

We can all have a great life!

To Lead a powerful, influential and great life;
consider:

1. Vision - Seeing with your mind's eye where you
want to be and what you want in life.
2. Discipline - paying the price to bring the vision into
reality. Doing whatever it takes to make things
happen.
3. Passion - fire, desire, and drive that sustains the
discipline to achieve the vision.
4. Conscience - inner/ inward guiding force to vision,
discipline and passion. i.e your spiritual life.

These 4 involves everything needed to live life lively!

Enjoy Today

08 July

Good Morning!

"I have come that they may have life, and that they may have it more more abundantly" - (John 10:10b).

With Jesus, you can enjoy life to the fullest!

Enjoy Today

09 July

Good Morning!

I want to share with you the summary of a sermon I listened to yesterday on Facts about Life of by Pastor Paul Enenche.

The 5 points below was discussed.

1. Life is a Gift - live it to the pleasure of the Giver, God.
2. Life is a Privilege - don't take it for granted. Live with appreciation.
3. Life is a Seed - daily living is sowing, that will produce a harvest. Sow good seeds.
4. Life is a Game - Play to Win.
5. Life is Vapour - Live everyday as if it's the last. Don't bother with what does not matter!

What a true message. Enjoy Today

10 July

Good Morning!

Your Help is with God
Your Future is with God
Your Direction is with God
Your Provision is with God
Your Honour and Dignity is with God
Your Eternity is with God!

Look up to God!
You are blessed!

Enjoy Today

11 July

Good Morning!
You are Unlimited!
The only limits on your life are those that you set
yourself!
You have more than you think inside of you.

Enjoy Today

12 July

Good Morning!

"When you Begin to Change the way you look at Things, Things will Begin to Change the Way They Look" – Dr Cindy Trimm

Be Optimistic!

Enjoy Today

13 July

Good Morning!

Today Matters!
Don't put off till tomorrow what you can do Today! Enjoy Today

14 July

Good Morning!

'I will praise You, for I am fearfully and wonderfully made; marvellous are Your works, and that my soul knows very well'. (Psalm 139:14).

You are Beautiful
You are Attractive
You are Valuable

You are God's Masterpiece
You are God's most priced possession

You are Royalty
You are Special
You are Complete
You are Perfect
You are Whole
You are Outstanding

Enjoy Today

15 July

Good Morning!

A Journey of one thousand miles begins with a step!
We grow great by degrees
Small victories lead to large victories
Build on the small to achieve the great
Start Today

The first day of the rest of your Life!

Enjoy Today

16 July

Good Morning!

1. KNOWLEDGE is your Greatest Asset.
Grow in knowledge, wisdom and understanding by reading daily.
Acquire new knowledge and information daily that enlightens and serves you.
Remember to apply what you learn, as only Applied Knowledge is Power!

2. TIME is your most Valuable Asset.
Time is the most precious commodity. Use it Wisely! 'Time is Money'! How productive are you? Can you look back and account for what you did with 24 hours yesterday, last week, last month, and last year? Be Time conscious! Time slips through our hands like grains of sand, never to return. What separates 'the successful' from 'the unsuccessful' is the way they use time.

3. RELATIONSHIPS are your most Cherished Asset!
Maintain intimate fellowship with God on a daily basis.
Associate with the right people, i.e those who will lift you up and not those who will drag you down.
Maintain good relationships with your close family, at all costs. At the end of life, they are the ones that will surround your bedside!

Master these 3 Principles and you MASTER LIFE!
Enjoy Today

17 July

Good Morning!

No Pain, No Gain.
You must sacrifice the Present Pleasure for the Future
Good!
Push Yourself to the Limit!
It's called Positive Pressure. Pressure is needed to
Achieve a bit more than the day before!
Keep moving, keep building and keep making progress!
Enjoy Today

18 July

Good Morning!

You are a Victor!
You are victorious!

Don't be a Victim!
A Victim is one who walks on a beach and sees sand as
dirt!
A Victor sees the sand as an ingredient for building a
castle!

The way you view the world and see your life shapes
your life! Enjoy Today

19 July

Good Morning!

"There are 3 categories of people in Life:
1. Those who make things happen
2. Those who watch things happen
3. Those who say, what happened?" – Robert Kiyosaki

Where do you belong?

Enjoy Today

20 July

Good Morning!

Success on the Outside Begins with Success on the
Inside!
Your attitude and approach determines your results!
Enrich your (mind) inner world; and your outer world
will be enhanced.
The quality of your life is determined by the quality of
your thoughts.

Enjoy Today

21 July

Good Morning!

Be Bold
Be Strong
Be Fearless
Be Confident
Be Courageous!

Enjoy Today!

22 July

Good Morning!

Life is about growth!
To live is to be growing daily!

'No matter how far you have gone in life, there is always a place called FORWARD'

Keep moving, Keep growing, Keep expanding!

Enjoy Today

23 July

Good Morning!

Life is good.
Don't stop dreaming!
Never lose hope
Don't worry about your weaknesses
Focus on your strengths

Enjoy Today

24 July

Good Morning!

What you say to yourself is what you will see! Words are powerful!

Speak Creatively!

Speak Accurately!

Speak Positively!

Enjoy Today

25 July

Good Morning!

The gift of being alive is Priceless!

Only the living celebrate it!

Celebrate Life, Celebrate your Life!

Enjoy Today

26 July

Good Morning!

It's a Bright and Beautiful Day!

Embrace it with Gratitude!

Enjoy Today

27 July

Good Morning!

Time is your most valuable asset!
It is the most important and precious commodity!

When you manage your time, you manage your life!
Time mastery is Life mastery!

Use time wisely!

Enjoy Today

28 July

Good Morning!

A friend of mine forwarded this to me two weeks ago
and I think it's relevant message is worth sharing:

While a man was polishing his new car, his 6 yr old son
picked up a stone and scratched lines on the side of
the car.
In anger, the man took the child's hand and hit it many
times; not realising he was using a wrench.

At the hospital, the child lost all his fingers due to
multiple fractures.

When the child saw his father...

With painful eyes he asked, 'Dad when will my fingers
grow back?'

The man was so hurt and speechless; he went back to
his car and kicked it a lot of times.

Devastated by his own actions.....sitting in front of that car he looked at the scratches;
The child had written 'LOVE YOU DAD'

The next day that man committed suicide. .

Anger and Love have no limits;

Choose the latter to have a beautiful, lovely life.....

Things are to be used and people are to be loved. But the problem in today's world is that, People are used and things are loved.

Let's be careful to keep this thought in mind:

Things are to be used, but People are to be loved.

Enjoy Today

29 July

Good Morning!

Is there a huge difference between Existing and Living?

Yes there is!

This is my take on it: Both are equally important, as without existence, there is no living. But living reflects how well we utilise our existence!

So the point is - Don't just exist, Live!

Enjoy Today

30 July

Good Morning!

If you could turn back the hands of time, what would you do differently?

This powerful question was raised in a movie I watched yesterday called 'Soul Tie'. The answers and insight the question provided led to the revival of a relationship that was at the verge of breaking down.

It really got me thinking about my life too!
I believe the 'Past is in the Past' and we learn and grow from mistakes.
I also believe totally that things happen for a reason which may not make any sense at the time.

I don't like the word regret - it gives negative vibes which sometimes prevent logical reasoning. So I see everything as experiences with lessons to learn and note that there are better choices that could have led to more favourable outcomes.

So yes there are a number of things that could have turned out differently if I had considered my choices.

I would never be able to turn back the hands of time; so NOW in every situation I will consider better choices and not repeat an unpleasant experience. I will prayerfully and thoughtfully consider all my Decisions and Choices!!

What does all this mean to you?

If you could turn back the hands of time, what would you do differently?

Enjoy Today

31 July

Good Morning!

When you do the right thing;
When you do things right; things always work out right.

Be a Person of Principle!

Enjoy Today

8
AUGUST – BELIEVE IN YOURSELF

01 August

Good Morning!

The times of the day can be likened to different phases
of our Life:
Morning: before age 30
Mid Day/ Afternoon: 30 to 50 years
Evening: 50 to 70 years
Night time: 70 and above

The morning time of the day is our years before age
30. The morning of Life!
The Morning is the time to Wake Up, Arise, Get out of
bed, Set a Solid Foundation and Prepare for the Day.
The earlier you wake up, the better!

The Foundation we set in the morning phase of our life
determines how strong or weak the building will be.
The morning mostly sets the pace for the rest of the
day. It's the Preparation and Foundation Phase. There
are Important things that are meant to be done only in
the morning. Some people miss out on the morning
phase because they sleep well into midday.

All times of the day is just as full of meaning as the

morning; each meaning and purpose are different.

Enjoy Today

02 August

Good Morning!

The Mid Day and Afternoon Phase of Life is between 30 and 50 years.

It's the Building Phase! What you build and how you build depends on the skills, knowledge and habits acquired during the foundation and preparation stage. It's the time to build, gain momentum, create and add meaning to the world and yourself. During this phase, especially in the late afternoon one comes to the realisation that Life is not something that has meaning but it's something we give meaning to!

The Focus moves as you progress through this phase from ambition, success and achievements to adding value to the lives of others and enjoying meaningful experiences! You will only be able to give what you have! If there is nothing of value in ones life, there will be nothing to give. Issues develop when people cannot find meaning to Life, and feel there is something missing, usually referred to as 'mid-life crisis'. Purpose becomes crucial in this phase of life!

To be continued.......

Enjoy Today

03 August

Good morning!

Extracts from the Book - 'The Four Agreements' by Don Miguel Ruiz.

It encourages us to adopt these 'four powerful agreements' that will help break other agreements (false beliefs) that come from fear and snap our energy.

1. Be Impeccable with Your Word - Your word can create or destroy, it can build or pull down. Do not use your word against yourself! Simply put, speak positively, creatively and accurately!

2. Don't Take Anything Personally - nothing other people do or say is because of you, it is because of themselves! Others have opinions according to their belief system, so nothing they think or feel about you is really about you, it's about them!

3. Don't Make Assumptions - we all see life differently. Making assumptions causes difficulties and creates a false image!

4. Always Do Your Best - When you work because you feel you have to, you are not working at your best. Working because you want to do it, and not because you have to, makes you work at your best. Your best manifests when you are enjoying the action or doing it in a way that will not have a negative impact on you e.g. frustration and unhappiness.

Make a positive agreement with yourself! Enjoy Today

04 August

Good Morning!

Purpose is the Reason for the Journey of Life; Passion is the Fire that lights your way

It's your road and yours alone. Others may walk it with you, BUT no one can walk it for you.

Enjoy Today

05 August

Good Morning!

The story is told of a father who takes his son into the forest, blindfolds him and leaves him alone. He is required to sit on a stump the whole night and not remove the blindfold until the rays of the morning sun shine through it. He cannot cry out for help to anyone. Once he survives the night, he is a MAN!

He cannot tell the other boys of this experience. Each boy must come into his own manhood.
The boy was terrified, could hear all kinds of noise, beasts were all around him. Maybe even some human would hurt him. The wind blew the grass and earth, and it shook his stump. But he sat stoically, never removing the blindfold. It would be the only way he could be a man.
Finally, after a horrific night, the sun appeared and he removed his blindfold. It was then that he saw his father, sitting on the stump next to him; at watch the

entire night.

We, too, are never alone. Even when we don't know it, God is watching over us, sitting on the stump beside us. When trouble comes, all we have to do is reach out to Him
Moral of the story: Just because you can't see God, doesn't mean He is not there!

God is with you all the time!

Enjoy Today

06 August

Good Morning!

I received this from a friend recently and its a good one to share.
This story is on Focus: THE PREGNANT DEER!
Please read slowly and thoughtfully!

In a forest, a pregnant deer is about to give birth. She finds a remote grass field near a strong-flowing river. This seems a safe place. Suddenly labour pains begin.

At the same moment, dark clouds gather around above & lightning starts a forest fire. She looks to her left & sees a hunter with his bow extended pointing at her. To her right, she spots a hungry lion approaching her. What can the pregnant deer do?
She is in labour!

What will happen?
Will the deer survive?
Will she give birth to a fawn?
Will the fawn survive?
Or will everything be burnt by the forest fire?
Will she perish to the hunters' arrow?
Will she die a horrible death at the hands of the hungry
lion approaching her?

She is constrained by the fire on the one side & the
flowing river on the other & boxed in by her natural
predators.

What does she do?
She focuses on giving birth to a new life.
The sequence of events that follows are:
 Lightning strikes & blinds the hunter. He releases the
arrow which zips past the deer & strikes the hungry
lion.
 It starts to rain heavily, & the forest fire is slowly
doused by the rain.
 The deer gives birth to a healthy fawn.
In our life too, there are moments of choice when we
are confronted on all sides with negative thoughts and
possibilities.

Some thoughts are so powerful that they overcome us
& overwhelm us.

Maybe we can learn from the deer.
The priority of the deer, in that given moment, was
simply to give birth to a baby.
The rest was not in her hands & any action or reaction
that changed her focus would have likely resulted in
death or disaster.

Ask yourself,
Where is your Focus?
Where is your Faith and Hope?

In the midst of any storm, do keep it on God always.
He will never ever disappoint you. NEVER.

Remember, He neither slumbers nor sleeps...

Enjoy Today

07 August

Good Morning!

"You will also declare a thing,
And it will be established for you;
So light will shine on your ways" (Job 22:28).

Whatever you want to happen for you; say it, shout it
out, proclaim it, declare it, confess it and believe it!
I am Victorious
I am a Conqueror
I am Strong, Able and Calm!
I am so Grateful to God!
Enjoy Today

08 August

Good Morning!

Small things make a huge difference!
Be the Reason someone smiles today. Enjoy Today

09 August

Good Morning!

Relationships are important; however most are bound by time, level and purpose.
There are people God has placed throughout our journey in life, for a specific time and reason.

Sometimes they bring good, sometimes pain. God has a perfect reason for placing them in our lives.
Friends would only be friends until they have served their purpose in our lives. When their purpose is fulfilled, time for separation will set in and this could take different forms!
Remember people can and will always fail you, it's human nature! God never fails! It's Divine nature!

Enjoy Today

10 August

Good Morning!

"God grant me the Serenity (calmness) to accept the things I cannot change;
Courage to change the things I can, and Wisdom to know the difference" - Reinhold Neibhur.

The serenity prayer, as it is well known is one of the great ways to prevent stress, i.e. knowing the difference between what can and can't be changed.

Be blessed, not stressed.

Enjoy Today!

11 August

Good Morning!

Seek and you will find!! (Matt 7:7b)
Always Look for:
1. The good in every Situation. There always is!
2. The Valuable Lesson in every setback or difficulty.
3. The Solution to every Problem.

Enjoy Today!

12 August

Good Morning!

Its a Beautiful Day!
God makes everything Beautiful in its time
You are Beautiful
You have a Beautiful Life
It's what God says about you that counts.

Enjoy Today

13 August

Good Morning!

Don't be unsatisfied with your life. Many people in this world are dreaming of living your life.

A child on a farm sees a plane fly overhead and dreams of flying. But, a pilot on the plane sees the farmhouse and dreams of returning home.
That's life!! Enjoy yours!

Enjoy Today

14 August

Good Morning!

Fear is the biggest inhibitor to better things!

Ask Yourself: What would you do if you aren't afraid? Then go ahead and move in a new direction.

Enjoy Today

15 August

Good Morning!

"The purpose of life is a life of purpose" – Robin Sharma

Your Passion is your Purpose-----Pursue It!

Enjoy Today

16 August

Good Morning!

Today Matters!
It's a Gift from God
Be Grateful
Open it and Enjoy the Present!
Are you going to spend it, save it, share it or invest it?

Enjoy Today

17 August

Good Morning!

Morning Prayer:
"Cause me to hear your loving kindness in the morning, For in You do I trust; Cause me to know the way in which I should walk, For I lift up my soul to You". Psalm 143:8

Enjoy Today!

18 August

Good Morning!

Be grateful for your Life!
Make proper use of your time. Time management is
life management!!
Be the best you can be!
Don't live your life trying to impress others!
Don't make the same mistake twice!

Enjoy Today

19 August

Good Morning!

From struggle comes strength; and from pain comes
gain!
From disappointment comes appointment; from
displacement comes new placement!

We grow the most from our most challenging
experiences!!

Learn from your experiences.
To enjoy the utmost Joy of being on the summit of the
mountain, you must have first visited the lowest
valley!

Enjoy Today

20 August

Good Morning!

You are on a magnificent journey! The Journey of Life!!
Remind yourself how fortunate you are to be alive!
Keep Living
Keep Moving
Keep Going
Keep Doing
Keep Loving
Embrace Life! Enjoy Today

21 August

Good Morning!

Be Blessed, not Stressed! Enjoy Today

22 August

Good Morning!

Embrace Your Early Mornings.

Make it Meaningful.

Make it the most important part of all your Days!

Remember a Good life consists of good Days! Good

Days depend on Early Morning Routines, which helps start each day with Focus, Energy, Positivity and Confidence!

Enjoy Today.

23 August

Good Morning!

Do What You Can.
Effort is the only way to get Results!
The only impossible journey is the one you never begin!

Enjoy Today

24 August

Good Morning!

This is what you shouldn't do:
Don't Compare yourself to others
Don't Criticise yourself or others
Don't Compromise Yourself
Don't Condemn Yourself or others
Don't Complain about yourself or others.

This is what you should do:

Appreciate who you are and what you've got!

Enjoy Today

25 August

Good Morning!

Stand OUT don't Blend IN.
Believe in Yourself!

Enjoy Today

26 August

Good morning!

Key Life Skills:

1. Clarity: Have Clear Goals and Objectives. Write out your goals
2. Plan: Take steps to achieve them.
3. Action: Do something every single day that moves you toward your major goal
4. Visualise: think about your goals, review daily, focus on the outcome

There's a true story of a man who approached a labourer who was laying bricks and asked him, "what are you doing?" The labourer said, "can't you see I'm

laying bricks?"
The man then walked over to another bricklayer and asked, "what are you doing?" And the workman answered with pride, "I'm building a Cathedral".

Keeping the goal at your forefront, makes every task in your day and every step of your journey in life meaningful!

Enjoy Today

27 August

Good Morning!

There is always one thing to be thankful for every morning, to see the beauty of being alive under God's grace!

Enjoy Today

28 August

Good Morning!

Life is indeed Beautiful!

Celebrate Life

Enjoy Today

29 August

Good Morning!

Keep working on your goals!

It will well be worth it!

Remain Focused

Enjoy Today

30 August

Good Morning!

There are so many challenges in and around the world right now.

There is Peace within and I pray you experience it.

Enjoy Today

31 August

Good Morning!

Pain is part of life!

There are 2 types of pain; pain on the road to success or pain of being haunted with regrets.

Step out and make wise use of Today

Enjoy Today

9
SEPTEMBER – BE PREPARED

01 September

Good Morning!

Glory to God Almighty!
Welcome to September.
It's a New Day
It's a New Dawn
It's a New Month
It's Newness!
To experience New, and Better Results; we must
change what we do and how we do it! We can't keep
doing the same thing over and over again and expect a
different outcome.

It's not what we do once in a while that shapes our
lives, but what we do consistently. For long term
maximum beneficial effects, we need consistent
effective habits. So make it a month of New Good
Habits!
Practice Good Habits Daily.

I like to refer you back to the message posted on 16
July.

1. KNOWLEDGE is your Greatest Asset.
Grow in knowledge, wisdom and understanding by reading daily.
Acquire new knowledge and information daily that enlightens and serves you.
Remember to apply what you learn, as only Applied Knowledge is Power!

2. TIME is your most Valuable Asset.
Time is the most precious commodity. Use it Wisely!
 'Time is Money'! How productive are you? Can you look back and account for what you did with 24 hours yesterday, last week, last month, and last year? Be Time conscious! Time slips through our hands like grains of sand, never to return. What separates 'the successful' from 'the unsuccessful' is the way they use time.

3. RELATIONSHIPS are your most Cherished Asset!
Maintain intimate fellowship with God on a daily basis.
Associate with the right people, i.e those who will lift you up and not those who will drag you down.
Maintain good relationships with your close family, at all costs. At the end of life, they are the ones that will surround your bedside!

Enjoy Today!

02 September

Good Morning!

This is the simplest but most important Life Habit to develop!
Wake up Daily with an attitude of gratitude to God, your Maker and Creator.
As soon as you open your eyes, before you grab the phone you left under your pillow; that is if you were not holding on to it all night!
Before you tweet or send a message to the world; send a Thank you message to God first.
Appreciate God.
Acknowledge God.
Say good morning to God, sing to God, smile to God and speak to God.
Be grateful to be Alive!

Embrace every day with gratitude, joy and happiness!

Enjoy Today

03 September

Good Morning!

Practice Good Habits Daily.

Yesterday's message was about: Waking up Daily with an Attitude of Gratitude to God. If we do this, it signifies that we love, appreciate and acknowledge God.

"You shall love the Lord your God with all your heart,

with all your soul, and with all your mind" (Matt 22: 37)

"You shall Love your neighbour as yourself" (Matt 22:39). This is another very important Habit to practice and develop daily

Your neighbour is anyone that comes your way in your life's journey.

People Do Matter!

Life is not only about I, Me and Myself. Look around you and love the people God has placed in your life, starting with those close to you and in your household.

We love by doing small things Consistently:
Being considerate, Life does not evolve around you alone.
Pay compliments as and when necessary
Help where you can.
Show a little act of kindness,
Go Out of your way to make someone's day.
Be an extension of Gods Love and Light!

Start where you are, with what you have, use whatever God has given you to bless someone.
We all have something - even if it's the beautiful smile, and nice set of white teeth God has blessed you with to Smile; or the lovely voice or gifted hands. Use it to bless someone.
Be the reason someone smiles. Small things make a Huge Difference.

I like to illustrate how important each one of us is:
Imagine this scenario: it's your birthday and you wake

up in the morning excited. You see an envelope with your name on it.

Its a gift - the keys to your dream car. Just picture it in your mind, you go outside and parked is the very specific car you have always wanted, with your favourite colour ribbon; your dream car.

You can hardly believe it! Brand new bespoke luxurious leather interior fully loaded, full options with personalised car plate number. All yours with all the extras. Your parents are out of town, your siblings are not around. Feeling extremely excited, and keen to share the news; you take it for a spin round the block to show your best friend, but your friend was not there. You take a few photos and post it on Twitter & Instagram; there were no comments, no likes and no followers! You drive a few more miles with the roof top down to another friend's house; still no one shows. You called your 3rd friend and left a voice message on your way there.
You suddenly realise there is no one around, not a single soul on the streets of People's Boulevard to notice you and your dream car. You get to your 3rd friends house and there is no sign of anyone not even the dog!! You call your parents and got no answer. You drive a few more blocks to your Aunts house, you meet no one on the way and no one answers the door or the phone. All the excitement is drained. There is no one to share your dream with you. Where is everybody? You ask yourself.

Answer this honestly, do people matter?

Enjoy Today

04 September

Good Morning!

Practice Good Habits Daily:
1. Love God
2. Love your neighbour
3. Love Yourself.

Love yourself, Believe in Yourself and have confidence.
You Create Your Reality.
Your Dominant Thoughts, Words and Feelings provides
the pattern for which your world is fashioned!
Put differently, the subconscious accepts as true that
which you feel to be true!
So it is important to Think, Feel and Speak accurately
about oneself!

Finally Brethren, whatever things are true, whatever
things are noble, whatever things are pure, whatever
things are lovely, whatever things are of good report, if
there is any virtue and if there is anything
praiseworthy- meditate on these things (Phil 4:8).

An old Cherokee told his grandson, "my son, there's a
battle between two wolves inside us all.
One is Evil. It is anger, jealousy, greed, resentment,
inferiority, lies and ego.

The other is Good. It is joy, peace, love, hope,
humility, kindness, empathy, and truth."
The boy thought about it. And asked, "grandfather,
which wolf wins?" The old man quietly replied, "The
one you feed." Enjoy Today

05 September

Good Morning!

Are you practising Good Habits Daily?

Stephen Covey's 7 Habits of Highly Effective People:

Habit No 1- Be Proactive.

It means taking action and conscious control over your life, setting goals and working to achieve them.

To be proactive means instead of reacting to events as and when they happen, you create your own events. e.g. instead of working extra hard to resit a failed exam, you work hard, plan, and take proactive steps to prevent failing the exam in the first instance.
You are responsible for your own happiness and most of your circumstances!!

Wishing my Sister Eunice, happiness always as she celebrates her birthday this day!

Enjoy Today

06 September

Good Morning!

Practice Good Habits Daily!

Stephen Covey's 7 Habits of Highly Effective People:

Habit No 1- Be Proactive.

Habit No 2 - Begin With the End in Mind.

Have a clear understanding of your destination, so that you better understand where you are now; and so that the steps you take are always in the right direction.

Have clear written goals and objectives.
Have an action plan to achieve them.
Visualise and focus on the outcome.

You cannot hit a target you can't see!

Enjoy Today

07 September

Good Morning!

Practice Good Habits Daily!

Stephen Covey's 7 Habits of Highly Effective People:

Habit No 3 - Put First Things First

Get your Priorities right!
Focus your time on highest priority activities that take you a step closer to achieving your goals and dream.

Use the ABCDE method: Review your all your activities daily and put an A, B, C, D, E next to each item.
A: something that you must do. It has serious positive or negative consequences if you do it or fail to do it. e.

g. Attending classes, praying, going to work, studying, reading
B: something that you should do. Has mild consequences. e. g. Attending weekly training/ fit sessions, saving etc
C: would be nice to do but have no consequences if you do it or not. e.g. meeting a friend for lunch
D: tasks that you could delegate or defer to free up more time for the 'A' tasks that only you can do.
E: something you can Eliminate altogether and won't make any real difference. e.g. watching TV especially crap programmes that add no value to your life

Focus more of your time on 'A' activities.

Enjoy Today

08 September

Good Morning!

Stephen Covey's 7 Habits of Highly Effective People:

Habit No 4:
Think Win-Win!

Let your philosophy when dealing with other people be: Mutual Benefit.

Relate to other people with integrity, maturity and abundance mentality. It's not about 'my way' or 'your way'; it's about a better way, a higher way!!

Have a Win-Win Mindset: Believe that everyone can win and constantly seek mutual benefit in all human interactions!

Enjoy Today

09 September

Good Morning!

Stephen Covey's 7 Habits of Highly Effective People:

Habit No 5: Seek First to Understand then to be Understood!

Emphatic communication is important!

Be sincere, stay curious, be patient, listen, then speak.

One of the best ways to persuade others is with your ears - by listening to them.

Enjoy Today

10 September

Good Morning!

Practice Good Habits Daily!

Habit No 6: Synergise

To put it simply, synergy means "two heads are better

than one." Synergize is the habit of creative cooperation. It is teamwork, open-mindedness, and the adventure of finding new solutions to problems.

It is a process where people (in a team, family or group) bring all their personal experience and expertise to the table. Together, they can produce far better results than they could individually. Synergy lets us discover jointly things we are much less likely to discover by ourselves. It is the idea that the whole is greater than the sum of the parts. One plus one equals three, or six, or sixty--you name it.

When we begin to interact together genuinely, and are open to each other's influence, we begin to gain new insight. This allows creativity and the capability of inventing new approaches because of our differences. It is Powerful!

Valuing differences is the essence of synergy, it's what really drives synergy. Value the differences among people. Differences should be seen as strengths, not weaknesses.

Enjoy Today

11 September

Good Morning!

Stephen Covey's 7 Habits of Highly Effective People:

Habit 7: Sharpen the Saw

Sharpen the Saw is about self-improvement.
To illustrate: a woodcutter strained to saw down a
tree. A young man who was watching asked "what are
you doing?" "Are you blind?" The woodcutter replied.
"I am cutting down this tree." The young man said.
"You look exhausted! Take a break. Sharpen your
Saw." The woodcutter explained to the young man that
he had been sawing for hours and did not have time to
take a break.
The young man stated ..."if you sharpen the saw, you
would cut down the tree much faster."
The woodcutter said "I don't have time to sharpen the
saw. Don't you see I'm too busy?" That's what most
people say and do!!!!

How can you be too busy sawing with a dull blade???
A dull blade/ saw results in reduced output. Stop and
sharpen the saw!
Sharpen the saw means preserving and enhancing the
greatest asset you have - YOU!
It means having a balanced program for self renewal in
the four areas of your life: physical, social/emotional,
mental and spiritual.
As you renew yourself in each of these four areas, you
create growth and change in your life. Sharpen the
saw keeps you fresh, energised, vitalised, increases
your capacity for productivity and effectiveness. It
keeps you sharp, focused and strong.
However, it won't just happen. You have to take time
out DAILY to sharpen the saw, i.e. eat healthy,
exercise, rest, read, study, pray etc. it must become a
Habit!!
No one else can do this on your behalf! It takes
Discipline, Determination and Diligence!

To know and not to do is really not to know!

Enjoy Today

12 September

Good Morning!

There is greatness in you!
Every mind can develop greatness
It's God's purpose for us to become great and
successful
Our choices and decisions, however places us on one
of two roads in life.
One is the well - travelled road to mediocrity (average
or ordinary), the other road is the road less travelled to
Greatness!

Dare to be different; take the road less travelled!

Enjoy Today

13 September

Good Morning!

God is our Strength and Refuge; A very present help in
time of need (Psalm 46:1).

Don't Give up
Don't Give in
Don't Give out

Enjoy Today

14 September

Good Morning!

You are Beautiful, Wonderful and Valuable
Don't seek to be like anyone or others
Everyone is different.

Be Yourself

Enjoy Today

15 September

Good Morning!

A Great Poem, extracted from Napoleon Hill's book

If you think you are beaten, you are,
If you think you dare not, you don't,
If you like to win, but think you can't,
It is almost certain you won't.

If you think you'll lose, you are lost
For out of the world we find,
Success begins with a person's will
It is all in the state of mind.

If you think you are outclassed, you are,
You've got to think high to rise,
You've got to be sure of yourself before You can ever

win a prize.

Life's battles do not always go
To the stronger or faster man,
But soon or late the man who wins
Is the one WHO THINKS HE CAN!

Enjoy Today

16 September

Good Morning!

Do you know who you are?
You are Amazing!
You are God's MasterPiece
Don't compromise who you are!

Enjoy Today

17 September

Good Morning!

You are Empowered!
You are Equipped for success!!
Go ahead and fulfil your destiny
Be all that God has created you to be!
"I can do all things through Christ who strengthens
me" (Phil 4:13).

Enjoy Today

18 September

Good Morning!

Your habits becomes your character;
and your character creates your destiny!

Are you daily practicing good habits?

Enjoy Today

19 September

Good Morning!

Life is Dynamic, not Static!
Growth is the essence of existence!!
Are You growing?

Your future is of your own making
The only way to improve Tomorrow is to know what
you did wrong Today!!!
Daily personal reflection helps you make improvements
which will enhance your growth!

Enjoy Today

20 September

Good Morning!

Appreciate Today!
Today matters!
Look forward to Tomorrow BUT take time to enjoy the beauty of Today!
Look forward to your life ahead BUT take time to embrace the wonders of living the moment!
Don't hurry through Today; don't rush through life; take time to see and experience all that's good along the way!
Happiness is a journey not a destination!

Enjoy Today

21 September

Good Morning!

"He who knows and knows that he knows is wise; Seek him.
He who knows and knows not that he knows is asleep: Wake him
He who knows not and knows that he knows not is a child; Teach him
He who knows not and knows not that he knows not is a fool; Avoid him" – Chinese Proverb.

Wisdom is the principal thing, therefore get wisdom; and in all your getting; get understanding (Prov 4:7).

Be Wise! Enjoy Today

22 September

Good Morning!

This is the day the Lord has made; we will rejoice and be glad in it (Psalm 118:24).

TODAY
Is a Gift, a Present from God; Beautifully wrapped and well presented!
Lord I accept the Precious Gift of Today. I open it, and choose to use it wisely.
I will enjoy the contents (blessings) and use the opportunities that come my way to show kindness, Love and do good. I am grateful and will continue to thank You Lord for every moment!

Enjoy Today

23 September

Good Morning!

It's a Brand New Day.
I'm Grateful to God for my Life!
I'm Grateful to God to be Alive!

Please Take TIME to READ this. It was forwarded to me 2 weeks ago and it is definitely worth sharing!

Lessons of life.........

A man died...

When he realized it, he saw God coming closer with a suitcase in his hand.

Dialog between God and Dead Man:

God: *Alright son, it's time to go*

Man: So soon? I had a lot of plans...

God: *I am sorry but, it's time to go*

Man: What do you have in that suitcase?

God: *Your belongings*

Man: My belongings? You mean my things... Clothes... money...

God; *Those things were never yours, they belong to the Earth*

Man: Is it my memories?

God: *No. They belong to Time*

Man: Is it my talent?

God: *No. They belong to Circumstance*

Man: Is it my friends and family?

God: *No son. They belong to the Path you travelled*

Man: Is it my wife and children?

God: *No. they belong to your Heart*

Man: Then it must be my body

God: *No No... It belongs to Dust*

Man: Then surely it must be my Soul!

God: *You are sadly mistaken son. Your Soul belongs to me.*

Man with tears in his eyes and full of fear took the suitcase from the God's hand and opened it...

Empty...

With heartbroken and tears down his cheek he asks God...

Man: I never owned anything?

God: *That's Right. You never owned anything*.

Man: Then? What was mine?

God: your *MOMENTS*.
Every moment you lived was *yours*.

Life is just a Moment.

Do Good in every moment
Think Good in every moment
Thank God for every moment

Live it...

Love it...
Enjoy it......

Enjoy Today

24 September

Good Morning!

'If you don't know where you are going, how will you know when you get there'!!

It's extremely important to set goals!

Clearly written defined goals serves as a guidance, and helps you move in the right direction on your life journey.

Keep it simple and short.
Preferably use a pen and paper and not electronic gadgets.
Place it where only you can see it daily or write it in a small pocket book named goals/ dreams book.
This stuff works!
Set yourself spiritual goals, academic / career goals, financial goals, personal empowerment goals, social goals, relationship goals, physical fitness goals etc; depending on want you want out of life!
If you want something, go get it!
1. Set the goal or objective
2. Give it a deadline - short term or long term
3. Formulate a Plan - to include the actions to be taken
4. Carry out daily or weekly activities as necessary

towards fulfilling the goals.
5. Review and evaluate your progress regularly.

Knowing your goals, objectives and aims helps you to keep on track, and manifest your vision into reality by a structured plan & consistent action!

One day Alice came to a fork in the road and saw a Cheshire Cat in a tree. "Which road do I take?" She asked. His response was a question: "Where do you want to go?" "I don't know," Alice answered. "Then," said the cat, "it doesn't matter."
(Lewis Carroll, Alice in Wonderland).

Enjoy Today

25 September

Good Morning!

'We must become the change we seek in the world' - Gandhi.

Enjoy Today

26 September

Good Morning!

Be inspired.
Be passionate
Passion is the fire that fuels your dreams.

Remember that 'what lies behind you and what lies in front of you is nothing when compared to what lies within you'!

Be Bold
Be Courageous
Be Confident
Be Fearless
When you conquer your fears, you conquer your life!

"For God has not given us a spirit of fear, but of love, of power and of a sound mind" (2 Tim 1:7).

Enjoy Today

27 September

Good Morning!

"This Book of the Law shall not depart from your mouth, but you shall MEDITATE in it day and night, that you may observe to do according to all that is written in it. For then you will make your way prosperous, and then you will have good success". (Joshua 1:8).

Don't forget your MAP today or any day.

MAP: Meditation, Affirmation and Prayers (MAP) - Your daily Guide for life's Journey!

28 September

Good Morning!

I am Grateful for my Life!
I am Grateful to be Alive!
Today is a Great Day!

Our Thoughts and Words affect the mind in a
pronounced way.
Out thoughts, including written or spoken words, are
powerful influences.
While what you say to others is important, even more
important is what you say to yourself.
Affirm Yourself!
Make Positive Affirmations!

Your Day and Your Life is greatly influenced by what
you think and say about Yourself!

Enjoy Today

29 September

Good Morning!

Don't make a big deal out of something that's not a big
deal!

Be blessed, not stressed!

Enjoy Today

30 September

Good Morning!

Wherever you are in the world; put a smile on your face and be grateful.

Remember some people never made it through the night!

Enjoy Today

10
OCTOBER – BE PHENOMENAL

01 October

Good Morning!

Embrace this New Month with a heart of gratitude, a positive attitude and fortitude!

Don't Quit!
A Winner never Quits and a Quitter never Wins!

Enjoy Today.

02 October

Good morning!

Be a person that makes things happen! A person of decision, a person of action!
Feel the fear and do it anyway! Enjoy Today

03 October

Good Morning!

A Journey of One Thousand Miles begins with a Step!

The secret of getting ahead is getting started.
Just do it!

Enjoy Today

04 October

Good Morning!

"People often say that motivation doesn't last. Well, neither does bathing - that's why it is recommended daily" - Zig Ziglar.

Enjoy Today

05 October

Good Morning!

Your life is more about your future than your past!

Don't let your past mess up your future!

The world will look at you and what to define you from where you are coming from.
God looks at you and defines you from where you are going; and where He is taking you.

Move forward with God and chart a different course for your life!

Enjoy Today

06 October

Good Morning!

Success comes with a Price!

1. Denial
2. Diligence
3. Determination
4. Discipline

You must sacrifice the Present Pleasure for the Future Good!

There is no substitute for hard work!
At the counter of success, there are no discounts!
The price has to be paid in full.
Enjoy Today

07 October

Good Morning!

Celebrate your small Wins; it sets you up for big Wins!

Yesterday I was able to complete 1 minute 30 seconds of planks exercise. I have been on 1 minute for a few weeks. I also made progress during my swimming lesson. I said well done to myself.

Appreciate yourself.

Look yourself in the mirror and commend yourself for all the small efforts you make. Its powerful.

Enjoy Today.

08 October

Good Morning!

Challenges come not to obstruct, but to instruct!

Every event has a Lesson
Every experience offers you Lessons
Every circumstance comes loaded with lessons to be learnt

Our experiences fuel our inner growth

Open your mind to the learning in every event!

Remember, the mind is like a parachute, it works best when open!

Enjoy Today

09 October

Good Morning!

I pray that God's Presence goes ahead of you today and surrounds you always, that His Peace which surpasses all understanding abides with you; and His Power manifests in and through you. Amen! Enjoy Today

10 October

Good Morning!

"Life is like a bicycle; to keep a balance you have to keep moving" - Albert Einstein.

Keep Moving.

Enjoy Today

11 October

Good Morning!

'I have set the Lord always before me; because He is at my right hand I shall not be moved' (Psalm 16:8).

God is with you all the time.

Enjoy Today

12 October

Good Morning!

You will never know how great you are at something until you try.

Now is the time to do the thing you think you cannot do. Just Do it!

Enjoy Today

13 October

Good Morning!

"Nothing is impossible; the word itself says "I'm possible." - Audrey Hepburn.

Enjoy Today

14 October

Good Morning!

The Quality of your life depends directly on your choices!

Make Positive Choices
Make the Right Choices
Make Godly Choices!

Enjoy Today

15 October

Good Morning!

"You can do anything you set your mind to" - Benjamin

Franklin.

You really can do anything you set your mind to!
Success on the outside begins within!

Determination + Perseverance = Success.

Enjoy Today

16 October

Good Morning!

'Your Future is Created by what you do Today, not
Tomorrow' - Robert Kiyosaki.

Don't Procrastinate!

Enjoy Today

17 October

Good Morning!

The People you regularly associate with can influence
your life!
Choose your friends carefully.
Choose who you spend time with!

Associate with people who will lift you up, motivate you, challenge you to improve, stretch you to be the best, encourage you and add value to your life!

Be aware of people with negative energy and behaviours who always criticise, complain, compete, and contend!

If you hang around these people, not only will they snap all your positive energy, but you will soon become exhibiting similar behaviours.

Enjoy Today

18 October

Good Morning!
I received this recently and it's worth reading.

A girl bought an iPad, when her father saw it, He asked her "What was the 1st thing you did when you bought it?
"I put an anti-scratch sticker on the screen and bought a cover for the iPad" she replied.
"Did someone force you to do so?" "No" "Don't you think it's an insult to the manufacturer?" "No dad! In fact they even recommend using
a cover for the iPad" "Did you cover it because it was

cheap & ugly?"

"Actually, I covered it because I didn't want it to get damage and decrease in value."

"When you put the cover on, didn't it reduce the iPad's beauty?"

"I think it looks better and it is worth it for the protection it gives my iPad."

The father looked lovingly at his daughter and said, "Yet if I had asked you to cover your body which is much more precious than the iPad, would you have readily agreed???" She was mute.....

Indecent dressing and exposure of your body reduces your value and respect.

May God guide us all.

Enjoy Today

19 October

Good Morning!

Appreciate What You Are
You are Fearfully and Wonderfully Made!
Be all that God has created you to be!
Embrace Who You Really Are

You are God's Master-Piece; God created you Whole, Perfect and Complete.

Don't create a different you with overuse of beauty and

body enhancing products. Instead beautify the Real you: your inner self and mind. This is what will really matter at the end!!
Be You!

Enjoy Today

20 October

Good Morning!

Basically, we owe it all to God!
Gods Grace and Mercy is the reason we are alive
God's Power upholds us
God's Spirit directs us

Be Grateful to God
Be Grateful for Life
Be Grateful for God's Love!

Enjoy Today

21 October

Good Morning!

'The Pessimist sees Difficulty in every Opportunity. The

Optimist sees the Opportunity in every Difficulty.' - Winston Churchill.

Enjoy Today

22 October

Good Morning!

"Discipline is the Bridge between Goals and Accomplishment" - Jim Rohn.

Enjoy Today

23 October

Good Morning!

There is no app for Happiness!
Happiness is a Choice!
Choose to be Happy.

Enjoy Today

24 October

Good morning!

Learn where you are
You are where you are now for a reason.

You need it for where you want to be; and for where God is taking you. Be Present!

Enjoy Today

25 October

Good Morning!

"But by the Grace of God I am what I am..." (1 Cor 10:15)

My Hope is in You Lord - Psalm 39:7
My Strength comes from You Lord - Psalm 46:1
My Help comes from You Lord - Psalm 121:2
My Confidence is in You Lord - Psalm 16:8
My Blessing comes from You Lord - Proverbs 10:22
My Soul looks up to You Lord - Psalm 63:1
My Trust is in You Lord - Psalm 143:8
My Expectation is in You Lord - Psalm 62:5

Enjoy Today.

26 October

Good Morning!

Every day brings new choices!
You can either be positive or negative; an optimist or a pessimist.
Today and all days, choose to be an optimist.
It's all a matter of perspective!

Enjoy Today

27 October

Good Morning!

"Strength does not come from what you do. It comes from overcoming the things you once thought you couldn't do" - Unknown Author.

I came across the above quote yesterday in our Employee Social Club Newsletter. It's so profound and true, and just had to share it!

Enjoy Today

28 October

Good Morning!
"A candle loses none of its light by lighting another candle" – unknown author.

Be impactful! Make somebody smile.

Enjoy Today

29 October

Good Morning!

Cherish what you have
Thank God always for what you have had, and what you have now.
Thank God in advance, as He blesses you with what you will have.
Be Grateful!

Enjoy Today

30 October

Good Morning!

Don't wait for everything to be perfect before you decide to enjoy your life; because everything will never be perfect!

Start now!
It's simple - enjoy the simple things in life!

Enjoy Today

31 October

Good Morning!

There is a time and place for everything

This is the time to Arise and Shine!

Enjoy Today

11
NOVEMBER – BE ENCOURAGED

01 November

Good Morning!

Happy New Month!

Life is Beautiful!

Enjoy Today.

02 November

Good Morning!

Our minds assign dimensions. As a man thinks, so he is.
We create our own world through what we think, say and do!

Always think and say positive things to yourself.

Enjoy Today

03 November

Good Morning!

Focus on what matters most!

Pleasing God and not people!

Enjoy Today

04 November

Good Morning!

Choose Wisely!

Be careful to choose your friends, they can pull you down or elevate you!
Be careful to choose who you marry and spend the rest of your life with; he/she can make or break you!

Enjoy Today

05 November

Good Morning!

Yes I can!

'I can do all things through Christ who strengthens me' (Phil 4:13).

Keep Moving
Keep Going
Keep Moving Forward
Keep Moving Upward
Keep Making Progress

Don't let anything or anyone hold you back....

Enjoy Today

06 November

Good Morning!

When God is at the Centre of your life, you Worship. When He's not, you Worry!

Worry is the warning light that God has been shoved to the sideline.

Put God at the centre, and keep Him there through Worship. Enjoy Today

07 November

Good Morning!

What You Are (Character) is far more important than What you do (Career)!

As you are progressing in your career, remember to also develop good character qualities!!

Keep a firm grasp on BOTH Character and Career!

Enjoy Today

08 November

Good Morning!

The Journey is just as important as the Destination; so Live, Love, Learn and Laugh!

Enjoy Today

09 November

Good Morning!

Your thoughts, feelings and words are IMPORTANT!

Flick off negative thoughts, negative feelings and negative words!

Don't let anybody or anything determine how you feel, think, speak or act! Choose to be Happy.

Enjoy Today

10 November

Good Morning!

Your attitude of gratitude determines your altitude!
Be grateful to God!!
Be grateful for what you already have and you will attract more good things!

Begin each day with a grateful heart!

Enjoy Today

11 November

Good Morning!

Stop saying what you see, start saying what you envision!
Stop dwelling on your problems, start focusing on the opportunities to solve them!

The future is colourful!
Your future is bright!
Be Excited

Enjoy Today

12 November

Good Morning!

Each Morning is a Gift!

Each Morning is also a New Beginning!!

The Morning is the start to another exciting and great day!

Enjoy Today

13 November

Good Morning!

The future belongs to those who prepare for it!

Don't leave till Tomorrow what you can do Today!

Enjoy Today

14 November

Good Morning!

It's not great events that make great people; but great decisions!

Enjoy Today

15 November

Good Morning!

Happiness is a choice!
Be Happy!

Choose to be Happy
Let go of the pains of the past and the fears of the future

Accept the things you cannot change

Be grateful, appreciate every moment

Enjoy Today

16 November

Good Morning!

"Action is the Foundational Key to all Success" - Pablo Picasso.

One Action a Day is all it takes!

So what action will you take today that will get you closer to achieving your goals?

Enjoy Today

17 November

Good Morning!

Life is about Love!
Be passionate about life, about your Life and about living!

Fall in Love with your Life and Your Purpose!
Be Excited about who you are - A Child of God, Wife,
Husband, Parent, Child, Sibling etc you mean
something to someone, and you are impacting
someone's life. If that doesn't excite you, nothing will!

Be excited about what you do -your job, your career,
your interests or your hobby! You make a difference by
being productive!
Put your heart and soul into who you are and what you
do! Be excited about where your time and energy
goes!
Find pure joy in what you do!!
It does not really matter what you do, but it's
important to be passionate about it. There is nothing
like pure joy. It gives freedom and fulfilment!

Your passion should give you purpose and meaning! It
should motivate you to take action!

Enjoy Today

18 November

Good Morning!

Life is a Series of Days!

What you do first thing in the morning sets the tone
for the Day!
How Your Day starts often defines how your day goes!
Tips:
Use the early hours of the morning to kickstart your
day with Praise, Prayer and Power!

Start off on a Positive Note, Positive Attitude, Positive
Energy, and Positive Affirmations!

Enjoy Today

19 November

Good Morning!

If there is one quality that we all need more of to get
ahead in life, it's Confidence!

Nothing can stop you and affect your performance if
you:
Believe in yourself no matter what!
Believe in yourself to the extent that all fears,
uncertainty and doubts are gone!

Appreciate yourself, accept yourself for who you are and embrace your good qualities!
Be proud of who you are!
Respect and value yourself!
Approve yourself; don't wait for the approval of others!!

Enjoy Today

20 November

Good Morning!

Be Outstanding and ExtraOrdinary!
How?

Learn and Grow!
Growth is Key: improve yourself constantly - Personally, Spiritually and in all areas. Always be on the Grow!!

Work Hard!
Remember the 4 Ds! Refer to 06 October.

Stay Focused!
Keep your eye on the ball, your goals and your vision. Avoid discouragement and distractions!

Enjoy every moment! Enjoy the process of success unfolding!

Enjoy Today

21 November

Good Morning!

Life is about Living and Growing!

We Grow when we:
Stretch beyond our limits
Challenge ourselves.
Take on new opportunities
Take Risks. Some risks are worth taking.
Learn Something New - Expand our horizons.
Acquire Knowledge - keep learning, and invest in personal development

Conquer our fears
Leave our comfort zone!

Are you growing?

Enjoy Today

22 November

Good Morning!

Over the years, I have come across several motivational quotes; but I have 7 favourite ones! These quotes have stimulated me to take action and make changes in my life. I have lived them and they still do keep me in check!

I may have already quoted some or all of them in previous messages. However, I plan to share with you 1 quote everyday for the next 7 days. There is a story behind each quote!

But each day you receive the quote, I encourage you to read it over the course of the day and think about its true and deep meaning. Even if it's a familiar quote, think about how you can use it in your life to make positive changes.

My number one quote is one that my mother introduced me to in my very early years. She used to quote it regularly!!

I only JUST recently discovered the original author and source of the quote was one of the most extraordinary human beings the world has ever known. However, each time I read, recite or remember it; I hear my mum's voice. To me, she is the real author of that quote.

She taught me things I am finding more useful now in my life, decades after. I'm so grateful!
I dedicate this quote to my late mother. She was an

extraordinary woman; who raised and taught me well.

Here we go, my 7 favourite Quotes:
Quote Number 1:

"Do not put off tomorrow, what you can do today" -
Ben Franklin.

Enjoy Today

23 November

Good Morning!

I came across my 2nd favourite quote in 2013. It
helped me at a time when work and spiritual
commitments were overwhelming; finding balance and
fulfilment was a challenge.

The author is an incredible prayerful and powerful
Christian who walks her talk. She is also a well sought
after Motivational Speaker.

I used her Quote at the end of a 12 minute
presentation to an audience at work in June 2015. The
feedback received was so great!
One of the feedback States: 'I now have this quote
pinned above my desk at home". There were so many
more! It was an amazing feeling!

I love this quote. It is so very true!

Favourite Quote 2:

"When you begin to change the way you look at things, things will begin to change the way they look" - Dr Cindy Trimm.

Enjoy Today

24 November

Good Morning!

My 3rd favourite quote drives the point home that Time is Essence. It gave me a new perspective on life when I discovered it in July 2006.

The author has written so many books on money, finances, wealth, investment and real estate.
I have personally read 3 of author's books which I found enlightening!
I love this quote; and I hope you find it useful and meaningful as much as I did.

Favourite Quote 3:

"Your Future is created by what you do Today not Tomorrow" - Robert Kiyosaki.

Enjoy Today

25 November

Good Morning!

My Number 4 Favourite Quote is a very popular one by a Chinese Philosopher. Majority quote the latter part of this great quote, forgetting the first part of it. I sometimes think people miss the relevant message it aims to get across.

Quote No 4:
"Do the difficult things while they are easy and do the great things while they are small. A journey of a thousand miles begins with a single step" - Lao Tzu.

Enjoy Today

26 November

Good Morning!

My Number 5 favourite quote has a very deep meaning. I only hope you find it as you ponder on it. It's about thinking anew and developing a new mindset in order to manifest change!

There are other adapted versions of the quote, but still mean the same. It speaks volumes and I got a lot from it, looking at it from different angles. I'll let you make your own discovery!

No 5 Quote:
"You can't solve today's problems with yesterday's thinking" - Albert Einstein.

Enjoy Today

27 November

Good Morning!

My 6th favourite quote has a lot to say about planning and achieving!
So:

- What did you achieve this year?
- Did you set any goals?
- Did you plan?
- Did you take action?
- Did you make progress?
- What are your plans for the coming year?
- What will you do differently?

or are you just going to let one year keep rolling into another?

The Father of time management states in my No 6 Favourite Quote:

"Failing to Plan is Planning to Fail" - Benjamin Franklin.

Enjoy Today

28 November

Good Morning!

My 7th favourite quote places emphasis on Focus!
I always look in the direction of things that make me
feel joyful and happy.

The quote always reminds me:
- Of my point of attraction.
- to Look up to God
- to Set my mind on the things that I want to see
  happen in my life
- Not to be distracted from the ultimate picture.
- To pursue my goals relentlessly!

My Number 7 Favourite Quote:
"You will never reach your destination if you stop and
throw stones at every dog that barks" - Winston
Churchill.

Enjoy Today

29 November

Good Morning!

Be grateful for your life!
Remember not all that slept last night, made it through
the night!

'Through the Lords mercies we are not consumed, Because His compassions fail not. They are new every morning; Great is Your faithfulness' (Lam 3:22-23)

Please don't wake up angry, frustrated, with negative thoughts or depressed!

No matter what sort of day you had the day before; Embrace each day with a smile!

Enjoy Today

30 November

Good Morning!

Today is the Present, the Now and Here!

Yesterday is Gone, it's the Past, it's History!
It's pointless worrying about yesterday!
Tomorrow is the future, it's unknown, a mystery, not here!
Stressing about Tomorrow is not a good use of Today!

I have Today and I choose to be Happy!

Enjoy Today

12
DECEMBER – BE EMPOWERED

01 December

Good Morning!

It's a new Month!

"Life begins at the end of the comfort zone" – Neale Donald Walsch.
This month step out and do something new!

You have what it takes!

Enjoy Today

02 December

Good Morning!

I am all that God has created me to be!
I am created to prosper in all things!

"Beloved, I pray that you may prosper in all things and be in health, just as your soul prospers" - 3 John 2

I am Prosperous! Enjoy Today

03 December

Good Morning!

"Happiness can only exist in acceptance" - George Orwell.

Accept every Moment and make the best out of it!

Make the best of what you have!

Enjoy Today

04 December

Good Morning!

Learn from every experience
Don't make the same mistake twice
Be better and wiser next time!

Enjoy Today

05 December

Good Morning!

Don't settle for less than what you deserve!

You deserve the BEST!
You are Valuable!
You are Worthy

Enjoy Today

06 December

Good Morning!

Let go of the burdens of the past; it frees you to truly experience new things!

Enjoy Today

07 December

Good Morning!

Love who you are Today as you do something; to get a little better Tomorrow! Enjoy Today

08 December

Good Morning!

Trust in the Lord with all your heart;
And lean not on your own understanding; in all your
ways acknowledge Him and He shall direct your paths.
(Proverbs 3:5-6)

Enjoy Today

09 December

Good Morning!

God's word gives Direction in Life!

We need Gods word to light our ways, to give direction
for each step and wisdom for our plans.

Have you read God's Word lately?

"Your word is a lamp to my feet; and a light to my
path" - Psalm 119:105.

Enjoy Today

10 December

Good Morning!

All Glory to God Almighty!

We are Alive!
We are Standing!!
We are Well, We are Blessed!!

"This is the day the Lord has made, we will rejoice and be glad in it" - Psalm 118:24.

Enjoy Today

11 December

Good Morning!

Have you read God's Word lately?

"This Book of the Law shall not depart from your mouth, but you shall meditate on it day and night, that you may observe to do according to all that is written in it. For then you will make your way prosperous, and then you will have good success" - Joshua 1:8.

Enjoy Today

12 December

Good Morning!

"I can do all things through Christ who strengthens me" - Phil 4:13

Thank you Lord for Strength and Enablement

Go ahead and make a difference! Enjoy Today

13 December

Good Morning!

Connect with your Maker, the Almighty, the Creator of the Universe!

Have you thanked God lately?

'Rejoice always, pray without ceasing, in everything give thanks; for this is the will of God in Christ Jesus for you' - 1 Thes 5: 16-18.

Enjoy Today

14 December

Good Morning!

God's mercy and grace is the reason we are alive!

We owe it all to God!!

Have you acknowledged God lately?

"Through the Lord's mercies we are not consumed, Because His compassions fail not. They are new every morning; Great is Your faithfulness". - Lam 3: 22-23.

Enjoy Today

15 December

Good Morning!

There are 2 more weeks left in this year.

How prepared are you for the New Year?
Have you reviewed your goals?
Have you assessed your progress?
What things do you need to change?
What areas of your life need improvement?
What old things and old habits do you need to get rid

of, to allow newness?

What burdens and baggage (unforgiveness, anger and all inappropriate behaviour) do you need to drop so you can move forward?
Wake up, do the right thing, do things right and right every wrong.
Don't go into the New Year with the wrong attitude and approach!

Enjoy Today

16 December

Good Morning!

I am grateful to God for Life.

"I lay down and slept; I awoke, for the Lord sustained me" - Psalm 3:5.

Enjoy Today

17 December

Good Morning!

Go ahead and be all that God has created you to be!

Enjoy Today

18 December

Good Morning!

Make your life meaningful.
Let your actions help and inspire others!

Make a difference!

Enjoy Today

19 December

Good Morning!

Peace is the highest Happiness!

Peace of mind is the ultimate! It can't be bought!

'The Peace of God which surpasses all understanding

will guard your hearts and mind through Christ Jesus' -
Phil 4:7

Jesus is the Prince of Peace!
Connect with Him as you celebrate Christmas!

He is the reason for the season!

Enjoy Today

20 December

Good Morning!

Glory to God, it's been a fabulous Year!

I still have a lot I can improve on and it reminds me of
a quote:
'No matter how far you have gone in life, there is
always a place called Forward'.

Enjoy Today

21 December

Good Morning!

Don't Give up, Don't Give in, Don't Give out, Don't Give
Down, Don't Give.

There is a New Year around the corner!

Enjoy Today

22 December

Good Morning!

The future is colourful

Your Future is colourful! Enjoy Today.

23 December

Good Morning!

There is greatness in You!

Enjoy Today

24 December

Good Morning!

You are Blessed, not Stressed!

Enjoy Today

25 December

All I have to say is Thank You Lord

Wishing you a Merry Christmas and a Wonderful New Year Ahead!

Enjoy Today

26 December

Good Morning!

We need to keep moving upward, moving forward, increasing, growing and expanding!!

How have you done this Year?

Regardless of what's happened, be expectant.

Be determined and look forward to a New Season of Prosperity, Health, Fulfillment, Joy and Abundance. Enjoy Today

27 December

Good Morning!

You are a Radiant Being!

Shine brightly to God's Glory. Enjoy Today

28 December

Good Morning!

Harmony, Peace, Love and Joy indwells you.

You are Blessed

Enjoy Today

29 December

Good Morning!

Bless the Lord o my soul and all that is within me bless His Holy name! Enjoy Today

30 December

Good Morning!

"The end of a thing is better than it's beginning" – Ecc 7:8

Glory to God for a great end to a wonderful Year!

Enjoy Today

31 December

Good Morning!

The start of a new calender year provides a time for reflection and a planned opportunity to make changes. Make necessary changes for improvement.

Have a Happy New Year!

See you in the New Year. Amen
Enjoy Every Day
Enjoy Each Moment. Enjoy Today.

AYOOLA KAFFO

ACKNOWLEDGEMENTS

Thanking God for His Grace and Mercy. I take it not for granted. I thank God for my Journey so far.

Thanking God for my Husband, Mr Razaq Olukayode Kaffo. My Hero and my sweetheart. You are my Sweet at Heart! I thank God for you.

Thanking God for blessing me with 'OneFamily' - My dad, two loving sisters and my 'brother', nieces, nephews and Tanitoluwa. I love and appreciate you all.

Thanking God for my Spiritual Mentor, Pastor Bisi Dada. You are God sent and indeed blessed to be a blessing.

Thanking God for my Lovely Children – Femi and Kemi. You are my World. All my Love!

Thanking God for all my friends, family and the people He has surrounded and blessed me with.

Thanking God for Dr Dele Owolawi, being an author and writer of many books; your input, support and encouragement has been of tremendous benefit. Thank you Sir.

I am grateful to God for Pastors Dele and Moji Alabi. Their spiritual guidance and prayers helped me get back on my feet and to build my faith during a difficult period of my life between 2009 and 2011. Their ministry played a huge part in shaping me to be the person I am now.

To my late mother; may your soul continue to rest in peace. Your legacy lives on.

ABOUT THE AUTHOR

Ayoola is an experienced Occupational Health and Safety Specialist who enjoys reading, writing and presenting.

She has been a book reviewer since 2009. She started content writing in 2016 and officially an author in October 2017 with the short book **Live Life Lively: A to Z of Health and Success**; and this was immediately followed by **Enjoy Today: A Daily Inspirational Book**.

She is on a journey to be all that God has created her to be; and understands the importance of appreciating and cherishing each moment of her journey in life. She is very Positive, Proactive and Passionate about life and what she does; and she is keen to impact others positively.

Her books present an impactful and inspirational insight of living a successful, fulfilled and abundant Life.

Order your copy of other titles now via Amazon, https://www.amazon.com/author/ayoolakaffo

E-mail: akaffo@aol.co.uk

Printed in Great Britain
by Amazon

84107578R00130